MW01490342

DIABETES RENAL DIET COOKBOOK FOR BEGINNER'S

Delicious Dishes for All Stages of Kidney Failure. Meals Low in Sodium, Potassium, and Phosphorus. A Simple 35-Day Diet Plan.

DR. WILLOW MONROE

Copyright © 2022 - DR. WILLOW MONROE

All Right Reserved

The content contained within this book may be reproduced, duplicated or transmitted without direct written permission from the author or the publisher.

Under no circumstances will any blame or legal responsibility be held against the publisher, or author, for any damage, reparation, or monetary loss due to the information contained within this book, either directly or indirectly.

LEGAL NOTICE:

This book is copyright protected. it is only for personal use. You cannot amend, distribute, sell, use, quote or paraphrase any part, or the content within this book, without the consent of the author or publisher.

DISCLAIMER

Every effort has made this book as complete and accurate as possible. This book provides information only up to the publishing date. Therefore, this book should be used as a guide, not the ultimate source.

The purpose of this book is to educate. The author and the publisher do not warrant that the information contained in this book is fully complete and shall not be responsible for any errors or omissions. The author and publisher shall have neither liability nor responsibility to any person or entity concerning any loss or damage caused or alleged to be caused directly or indirectly by this book.

INTRODUCTION

You may be feeling anxious and helpless after receiving a diagnosis of kidney illness. Do not feel alone. Renal illness affects the lives of thousands worldwide. The good news is that there is a wealth of resources available to assist you in dealing with your health problem. This cookbook is designed to make the renal diet more manageable by giving you helpful hints and delicious meals. In spite of your kidney diagnosis, we hope you will find tremendous pleasure in preparing nutritious meals for yourself, your loved ones, and your friends with the aid of this cookbook.

In this cookbook, we will teach you how to do the following:

• The foundations of a renal diet

• How to prepare nutritious meals on a tight budget

•Recipes that are safe for those with renal impairment.

The renal diet is a special eating plan developed to assist people with kidney disease keep their organs functioning normally. Working with a certified dietitian to develop a renal diet that is right for you is essential due to the wide variety of renal diets available. The renal diet often lowers dietary consumption of protein, phosphorus, potassium, and salt. It's also recommended that you consume eight to ten glasses of water daily. The renal diet doesn't have to limit your culinary options at all. Every meal of the day is covered, from breakfast to dessert.

The protein, phosphorus, potassium, and salt content of all the dishes is rather modest. To assist you in preparing nutritious meals that are suitable for the renal diet, we have included a section on meal preparation and purchasing. We wish you success in controlling your renal health with the use of this cookbook and a lifetime of pleasure in the kitchen preparing nutritious, tasty meals for yourself and your loved ones. We wish you the best of luck in your efforts to adhere to the renal diet, and hope that the details presented here are useful to you. Keep in mind that before making any significant dietary changes, you should talk to your doctor or dietician. You may tailor your diet to your specific requirements and way of life with their help.

TABLE OF CONTENT

CHAPTER ONE

DIETS FOR RENAL FUNCTION

High protein content; renal disease may impair the body's ability to metabolize protein. If you have chronic kidney disease but don't need dialysis just yet, eating less protein may reduce the amount of waste products your body produces. People with end-stage renal disease (stage 5) are sometimes put on low-protein diets before starting dialysis or transplantation procedures, which involve accessing the peritoneal cavity (PD) or extracorporeal circulation (EC) via a catheter and a graft, respectively, three times a week at home or in a clinic for four hours each session.

High sodium levels are associated with hypertension, which may be reduced by limiting salt consumption, which also benefits the kidneys. The renal diet cuts down on salt by reducing consumption of processed foods that are rich in sodium and prohibiting the use of table salt. Flavor may be added without increasing sodium levels by substituting some sodium-free spices for salt. People with renal illness who have already lost a lot of function shouldn't take in more than two grams of potassium per day to prevent further cardiac complications.

Phosphorus is another mineral used by the kidneys in the process of purifying the blood. Dairy products and red meat, both of which are rich in phosphorus and may harm the kidneys, are off-limits on the renal diet. Enjoying these meals sometimes is OK, but you should not consume more than two portions of them in a single day.

Potassium content: Like phosphorus, too much potassium may be detrimental to your kidneys, thus it's important to minimize it on the renal diet. The maximum daily potassium intake on the renal diet is six grams, which is around 12 ounces of juice or three medium bananas. Fruits and vegetables, low-fat dairy products, and healthy grains are just few of the many delicious options that are low in potassium.

CHAPTER TWO

WHAT EXACTLY IS A RENAL DIET?

What exactly is a renal diet? There are many issues that may arise from kidney illness, but a "renal" or "kidney-friendly" diet can help preserve your kidneys and keep them functioning normally. Simple guidelines for sticking to the renal diet, together with tasty dishes for breakfast, lunch, supper, snacks, and dessert, are included in this comprehensive cookbook. Chronic kidney disease (CKD) and diabetic patients who practice healthy eating habits see considerable improvements in their conditions. Though there is a wealth of information at your fingertips, it may be difficult to decipher which meals are really beneficial to your kidneys. There are resources out there advocating for both high- and low-protein diets. Who therefore has the higher standard of evidence?

The renal diet is flexible and may be altered to meet the particular requirements of each patient. One of the primary tenets of the renal diet is to limit intake of salt, phosphorus, and protein in order to lessen the burden on the kidneys. Finding the right protein intake for you is more important than whether or not you have chronic kidney disease, so you may eat as much or as little as you want. Taking into account factors like your age, health, and lifestyle, a registered dietitian (RD) may assist you in developing a nutrition plan that is tailored to your individual needs.

What, then, is an appropriate diet for those with CKD? Listed below are some guidelines to get you moving in the right direction:

Select foods low in salt, such as fresh produce and whole grains. Try to limit your intake of processed foods like deli meats, canned soups, and frozen dinners since they often contain excessive amounts of salt.

Dietary phosphorus may be found in dairy products, nuts, seeds, legumes, and protein powders, all of which should be consumed in moderation. It might be difficult to totally limit your phosphorus consumption due to the prevalence of phosphorus-containing foods in the average diet; therefore, try to limit your intake by around 10% whenever feasible.

-Incorporate a variety of protein-rich foods into your diet, such as lean meat, chicken, fish, tofu, eggs, and legumes. Even if you have CKD, you still need to get enough protein in your diet to maintain muscle mass and repair damaged muscle tissue.

Don't eat or drink anything with added sugar or that's heavy in fat. Avoiding these junk foods will help you avoid gaining weight and experiencing other health issues.

Meals that are beneficial for your kidneys don't have to be bland and uninteresting just because you're following the renal diet. All of the dishes in this book are safe for anyone with renal disease and require little effort to put together. Healthy breakfasts like Pumpkin Oatmeal Pancakes and Berry Smoothie Bowls, as well as robust evenings like Turkey Meatballs with Quinoa Pilaf and Roasted Vegetables, are just a few examples of the wide variety of dishes that may be prepared. Dark chocolate brownies and apple crisp with cinnamon are just two examples of the desserts you may make at home. You may use this cookbook year-round to make nutritious and appetizing meals that are suitable for those with renal impairment.

STICKING TO THE RENAL DIET IS VITALLY IMPORTANT

Due to its potential to halt further kidney damage, the renal diet is crucial for those with kidney disease. Limiting certain foods in the diet helps ease the burden on the kidneys, which in turn protects them from further damage. When you adhere to a renal diet, you may improve your health and quality of life in general.

Some items to remember when on a renal diet are:

Avoid drinking as much water as possible. Juice, soda, coffee, tea, and alcohol should all be avoided or used in moderation. Be sure to discuss your daily fluid intake with your healthcare provider or Registered Dietitian.

Sodium, potassium, and phosphorus are three nutrients you should cut down on. Bananas, oranges, potatoes, sweetened yogurt, processed meat, and fast food should all be limited or eliminated from your diet.

You need to increase your intake of fruits and vegetables. This is a vital aspect of the renal diet because it ensures that you obtain enough of the right nutrients without eating too many calories. Reduce your intake of potassium, phosphorus, and salt by opting for these produce options.

The protein in your diet should come from a wide range of different animals and plants. You need protein because it contains amino acids that the body can't make. When looking for protein, choose for lean options like grilled chicken or fish, tofu, lentils, and eggs rather than fatty processed meats and dairy.

A healthy diet that includes enough of calcium is also important. Foods like cereals and orange juice, as well as fortified foods like milk and yogurt, include added calcium. In order to get the recommended daily allowance of calcium, a calcium supplement may be necessary for those with renal disease.

CHAPTER THREE

BENEFITS OF ADHERING TO THE RENAL DIET

The renal diet is a medically-recommended eating plan for persons with kidney disease or who are at increased risk for developing the condition. Kidney-harming foods and beverages are off-limits on the diet. In addition to limiting protein intake, a renal diet may also limit how much liquids, potassium, sodium, and phosphorus you take in each day. Renal diets are important because they may enhance kidney function and decrease the course of kidney disease. High blood pressure and diabetes, both of which are often seen in people with renal disease, may be avoided or kept under control with the right diet.

In spite of the numerous advantages of adhering to the renal diet, it is important to tailor the diet to your personal requirements. If you want to be sure you're getting enough of everything while still according to the rules of your specific renal diet, it's best to work with a registered dietitian who specializes in that area.

Kidney disease may be slowed with the renal diet, and in certain cases, kidney function can even be improved. Renal diet adherents also have a lower chance of developing hypertension and diabetes, two disorders that are often co-occurring with kidney disease.

The renal diet has several positive outcomes:

Kidney damage may be avoided or postponed with its aid.

It aids in the regulation of hypertensive levels.

The chance of developing heart disease is reduced.

Overall, it may make you feel better.

Consult your physician to determine whether the renal diet is right for you if you have kidney disease or are at risk for acquiring it. There are many of resources available to make sticking to the renal diet simpler.

Here are some fundamental guidelines to follow while embarking on the renal diet:

Reduce your consumption of foods rich in phosphorus, such as chocolate, nuts, legumes, and dairy products.

Try to stay off of drugs and alcohol.

Keep an eye on your salt consumption and aim to keep under the daily guidelines.

Fruits and vegetables should make up a large portion of your daily diet. They are a good source of vitamins and minerals and are low in phosphorus and potassium.

Maintain a healthy hydration intake; aim for eight 8-ounce glasses daily. In addition to being an essential element of the food, phosphorus is excreted from the body by drinking enough of water.

Consult with a certified dietitian who has expertise in renal diets to create a personalized eating plan. Renal diets have been shown to enhance kidney function and delay the course of kidney disease. If you want to be sure you're getting enough of everything while still sticking to the limitations your condition calls for, seeing a qualified dietician is a must. There are a wide variety of tasty dishes that adhere to the renal diet's food restrictions. Foods rich in phosphorus should be avoided or consumed in moderation, as should caffeine and alcohol, salt, and the lack of fresh produce. Be careful to get in your daily hydration intake; experts recommend a minimum of eight 8-ounce glasses of water. In addition to being an essential element of the food, phosphorus is excreted from the body by drinking enough of water.

CONSIDERATIONS OF THE RENAL DIET

Some drawbacks to the renal diet include:

All the rules about what you may and cannot consume might make it difficult to follow.

There is widespread agreement that the cuisine lacks flavor and appeal.

Buying all of the particular foods required for a renal diet may add up quickly.

Maintaining enough nutrition while on a renal diet might be challenging if you are not using locally sourced items in your cooking.

Despite these drawbacks, there are several advantages to sticking to a renal diet. It may also help reduce the advancement of renal disease, which may help keep your kidney function steady. If your doctor has recommended a renal diet, it is crucial that you stick to it religiously in order to get the most out of it. If you have any concerns about following your renal diet or need assistance coming up with new and tasty food ideas, it is recommended that you speak with your doctor or a qualified dietitian.

Not everyone has to follow the renal diet, but it may be an effective method of treatment for those who need. The best place to start when following a renal diet is a conversation with your doctor or a trained dietitian. With little ingenuity and hard work, you may enjoy a kidney-friendly diet that's also healthy.

There are a few things to remember if you're thinking about beginning a renal diet:

You should check with your physician to be sure this eating plan is appropriate for you. It's important to prepare ahead and be creative in the kitchen while following the renal diet.

Maintaining enough nutrition while on a renal diet might be challenging for those who are not used to cooking using regional foods. However, it is important to keep in mind that the renal diet is not the best option for everyone with kidney disease.

Consult your physician or a qualified dietitian if you've been put on a renal diet to learn how to make the healthiest possible dietary choices. Don't give up hope; with proper planning, a renal diet may be enjoyable and nutritious. You've got this!

People with kidney illness are often put on a special diet called the renal diet. The goal of this diet is to aid in the management of kidney disease symptoms and to delay the course of the illness. Protein is prioritized on the renal diet, whereas sodium, potassium, and phosphorus intake are restricted. There are limits on how much liquid and protein may be consumed daily.

Due to the many food and drink limitations, sticking to a renal diet may be challenging. There is widespread agreement that the cuisine lacks flavor and appeal. Maintaining enough nutrition while on a renal diet might be challenging if you are not using locally sourced items in your cooking.

Despite these challenges, there are several positive aspects to adopting a renal diet. It may also help reduce the advancement of renal disease, which may help keep your kidney function steady. If your doctor has recommended a renal diet, it is crucial that you stick to it religiously in order to get the most out of it. If you have any concerns about following your renal diet or need assistance coming up with new and tasty food ideas, it is recommended that you speak with your doctor or a qualified dietitian. Renal diets may be pleasant and healthful with a little creativity and planning.

CHAPTER FOUR

HOW TO MAKE THE MOST OF THE RENAL DIET

If you are having problems sticking to the renal diet, see your physician or a trained dietitian. They may make a diet plan that is simpler to follow since it is designed just for you. Reduce your intake of processed foods and replace them with whole foods. This will provide you a healthy dose of nutrients without the excess sugar and salt.

To add taste to your meal without increasing the sodium content, try cooking using low-sodium seasonings such herbs, spices, vinegar, and lemon juice.

-It's important to stay hydrated throughout the day, so try to drink at least eight glasses of water. Avoid caffeinated and alcoholic beverages in favor of water, unsweetened tea, and low-sodium vegetable juice.

-Smoking is very harmful to your kidneys, thus if you are a smoker, it is imperative that you give up the habit immediately.

Sodium, what is it, and how does it function in the body?

Sodium is a mineral that is abundant in the foods we eat every day. Most people think salt and sodium are the same thing. Sodium and chloride are both components of salt. Salt and other sodium-containing ingredients are common in home-cooked meals. Most processed foods have greater sodium levels because of the salt added during processing.

Sodium is crucial because it regulates fluid levels and impulse conduction throughout the nervous system. The improvement in muscular function and control of blood pressure are two additional benefits. But if you consistently take too much sodium, your body will have difficulties flushing it out. Hypertension, or abnormally high blood pressure, is a risk factor for cardiovascular disease and stroke.

Sodium, along with potassium and chloride, is one of the three primary electrolytes in the human body. Electrolytes are crucial for proper nerve transmission and muscular contraction, and they also control the influx and egress of fluids throughout the body's tissues and cells. In order for your body to operate normally, you need to keep your electrolyte levels up.

In what ways may I lower my salt intake?

You may lower your salt consumption in several ways, including as:

- Preferably eating whole, unprocessed meals as much as possible. The majority of fresh produce does not have any additional salt.

- Steering clear of processed meals, particularly salty options. Keep salt intake low by reading nutrition labels and selecting reduced-sodium options.

- Season your meal using herbs and spices rather than salt. Depending on your own tastes, you may choose from a wide variety of herbs and spices.

- Switching to a reduced-sodium kind of common table salt. Use potassium chloride salt or a reduced-sodium salt if you must add salt to your diet.

- Consuming several liquids on a daily basis. Sodium may be flushed out of the body in this way.

Why is it important for renal patients to limit salt intake?

Those with renal illness should avoid consuming an excessive amount of salt because their impaired kidneys cannot process the additional sodium and fluid. The accumulation of salt and fluid in the tissues and circulation has been linked to high blood pressure and cardiovascular disease.

Since sodium is an electrolyte, it plays a role in ensuring that cells have an appropriate ratio of water to salt. Sodium is also essential for the transmission of nerve impulses and the contraction of muscles. Hyponatremia, or low sodium levels, is frequent in persons undergoing dialysis or who have renal failure as a result of an imbalance between fluid retention and fluid loss as a result of dialysis therapy or drugs like diuretics (water pills).

They may lead to:

- Drier mouth

- Edema causes extremity and facial swelling.

- Elevated blood pressure

When the heart has to pump too much blood, it may become enlarged and feeble, leading to heart failure.

Having trouble breathing is a symptom of fluid building up in the lungs.

Confusion: alterations in mental state caused by an excess of fluids in the brain.

Convulsions: fluid buildup in and around the brain is a known trigger for these attacks.

Patients with renal illness should limit their daily salt intake to between 1500 and 2300 milligrams (mg), depending on their disease stage. A daily salt intake of 800 to 1600 mg may be necessary for those on dialysis. You may lower your salt intake by eating more fresh produce, healthy grains, lean proteins, and low-fat dairy products. While you shouldn't completely cut off your intake of high-sodium meals, moderation is key.

EXPLAIN THE FUNCTION OF POTASSIUM IN THE HUMAN BODY.

Potassium, a mineral, is created by the human body and is present in a wide variety of foods. Potassium helps keep the heart beating regularly and keeps its muscles working. The electrolyte and fluid balance of your blood depends on the presence of potassium. The kidneys help regulate potassium levels by flushing out excess and storing it for later use if levels drop too low. About 90% of the potassium in our body is stored in our cells, while the remaining 10 mq is found in the extracellular fluid.

The amounts of electrolytes like sodium and potassium are regulated by the kidneys, and they also regulate how much fluid is retained in the body. Alterations in the levels of these electrolytes may cause abnormal cardiac rhythm (arrhythmia) by disrupting the heart's electrical impulse. Patients with kidney disease or those undergoing dialysis must adhere to a renal diet that limits their consumption of potassium-rich foods. A renal diet is recommended for persons with chronic kidney disease (CKD), and this article will give some guidelines for sticking to this diet.

Good sources of potassium:

Bananas, avocados, cantaloupe, honeydew melons, kiwis, mangoes, nectarine, papaya, passion fruit, pineapples, and plums are all examples of fruits.

Artichoke hearts, beet greens, broccoli raab, cabbage, cauliflower, celery hearts, cucumbers, eggplant, garlic scapes, green beans, kale leaves, leeks, lettuce heads (cos or romaine), mushrooms (button or portobello), onions, peas (snow and snap), peppers (bell green, red, and yellow), pumpkin flesh (winter squash), radishes, scallions, shallot bulbs,

Cheese made using low-fat cottage milk

Meat and alternatives: lean sirloin steaks, chicken breasts without the skin and bones, fresh cod fillets cooked in a dry pan, center-cut lamb tenderloins, center-cut bacon cooked Canadian-style on the back or side of the roast, and center-cut turkey breast tenders.

Black beans, drained and canned; chickpeas, drained and canned; kidney beans, drained and canned; pinto beans, drained and canned; tofu, boiling without salt and firm; soybeans, mature and boiled; tofu, pressed.

For what reasons should those with renal disease limit their potassium intake?

When kidneys aren't working, they can't flush out the additional potassium, leading to a buildup of the mineral. Problems with the heart, weakness, and other symptoms are possible outcomes of hyperkalemia, a disorder characterized by unusually high blood potassium levels. In order to avoid hyperkalemia, patients with renal disease should restrict their potassium consumption.

Keeping tabs on your potassium consumption may be done in a number different ways:

Find out from your doctor the maximum amount of potassium you should consume.

Find out how much potassium is in a serving size by reading food labels.

Pick foods low in potassium on a regular basis.

Stay away from bananas, oranges, potatoes, tomatoes, and spinach, all of which are rich in potassium.

How can I prepare meals without using salt or other high-potassium foods?

In the kitchen, avoiding high-potassium items might be challenging, but not impossible. Numerous dishes may be prepared using foods that are low in potassium. Here is a selection of tasty dishes that renal patients may prepare:

Breast of chicken, baked

You may have a baked fish fillet with scrambled eggs and veggies (but not tomatoes or spinach) over a bed of cooked quinoa, couscous, rice, or pasta topped with red sauce and/or cheese.

I highly suggest this book if you have a passion for cooking but are at a loss as to how to begin preparing meals for someone who has renal illness and needs a low potassium diet plan. Since all of the recipes call for fresh fruits and vegetables rather than canned items, which tend to have high sodium levels, you may confidently prepare them for your loved ones without worrying about putting too much salt in their diet.

What should someone following a low-potassium diet eat?

People with kidney disease or other health issues, such as type 2 diabetes mellitus, need to keep a close eye on their blood glucose levels every day; this means that eating foods rich in fiber, like whole grains and fruits, can help stabilize one's sugar intake so that they do not experience spikes throughout the day while still getting enough sugar to function properly.

Tell me about phosphorus and its physiological functions.

Bones can't develop or stay healthy without the mineral phosphorus. Phosphorus is essential for the growth of bones, teeth, and organs, and it also aids in the proper functioning of muscles. After being digested and eaten, the phosphorus from food is deposited in the bones with the calcium.

When the body requires phosphorus for anything other than bone growth, such energy generation, it reabsorbs it from the bones. The kidneys filter out excess phosphorus in the blood by eliminating it in the urine. If your kidneys aren't working properly, your body won't be able to flush out extra phosphorus in the blood, and it might build up. If this happens, you put yourself at risk for hyperphosphatemia, or abnormally high blood levels of phosphate, which may have negative effects on your health. Those who suffer from chronic kidney disease (CKD) should strictly adhere to a renal diet that lowers their phosphorus intake. Maintaining healthy blood phosphorus levels while getting enough of the other nutrients necessary for optimal health is the purpose of a renal diet.

Milk and other dairy products (yogurt, cheese), meat (beef, chicken, pork), fish and seafood (salmon), nuts and seeds (almonds), legumes/beans like lentils or chickpeas, grains like wheat flour for bread & cakes), vitamin C-rich fruits, eggs & egg products, and foods with added sugars (candy bars, cookies, and other sweets) all contain phosphorus. The phosphorus in the food you consume is absorbed by your digestive system and carried through your circulation until the kidneys release it in your urine. Bones will hold the remainder. Renal tubule reabsorption occurs at physiologically optimal blood concentrations. Hyperphosphatemia occurs when the body has an excess of phosphorus and may lead to serious health issues including bone damage and renal failure (if ignored). An overabundance of this mineral in the circulation causes calcium to be drawn out of bones, making them weak, brittle, and finally completely breaking down, resulting to osteoporosis.

One of the most common complications of CKD is hyperphosphatemia, which occurs when the kidneys are unable to remove all of the phosphorus from the blood. This can lead to serious health issues, including cardiovascular disease, premature death (from heart attacks, strokes, etc.), and bone diseases. To maintain healthy blood phosphorus levels, a renal diet that reduces dietary phosphorus intake is recommended. Keep in mind that the objective of a renal diet is to provide enough nutrients while reducing phosphorus intake. If you want to find out what kind of diet might be ideal for you, go to a doctor or nutritionist.

There are many of meal plans available to help you stick to the dietary guidelines for phosphorus. Because of their reduced phosphorus content, milk and other dairy products may be a helpful addition to meal plans. Here's a breakfast idea that incorporates both milk and oatmeal:

Oatmeal Recipe for Morning Eats

Steel-cut oats, 3/4 cup skim milk, a dash of salt, optional brown sugar, and a teaspoon of vanilla essence. Directions:

In a medium saucepan, mix together the oats, milk, salt, sugar (if using), and vanilla extract (if using).

Over medium heat, stirring periodically, bring the mixture to a boil.

The oats should be soft and creamy after approximately five minutes of simmering over a low heat.

Eats just one.

This dish has less phosphorus than typical breakfast foods like eggs and bacon. Fish may also be part of a healthy diet since it is often low in phosphorus. Here's a salmon dish that's perfect for every meal of the day:

Salmon in a Creamy Yogurt Sauce with Herbs

One pound of skinless salmon fillet, lemon wedges (optional), and half a cup of plain yogurt seasoned with a quarter teaspoon each of dried dill and garlic powder. Directions: Get the oven ready by heating it up to 400 degrees. Using a small bowl, combine the yogurt, dill, garlic powder, salt, and black pepper. Spread the yogurt mixture over the salmon fillet in a baking dish. Cook for 20 minutes, or until salmon flakes easily. Makes plenty for four people.

These dishes are only a sampling of what may be made while adhering to a renal diet. It's important to talk to your doctor or a nutritionist about developing a diet plan that's tailor-made for you.

People with CKD, as well as those with diabetes or high blood pressure, must adhere to the renal diet since these illnesses may cause permanent damage to the kidneys if left untreated. You may help prevent or reduce the course of CKD by adhering to a renal diet and maintaining healthy phosphorus levels. Consult your physician about any dietary restrictions or eliminations they may recommend, and schedule frequent checkups to monitor your kidney function, blood pressure, blood sugar, and phosphorus levels.

CHAPTER FIVE

DIABETIC AND RENAL DIET BREAKFAST IDEAS

A renal diet might make morning meals more difficult. However, if you are attempting to reduce weight, it is extremely important to have breakfast every day. For a healthy and satisfying morning meal, try one of these suggestions.

Omelet with Veggies:

This omelet has a good balance of protein and phosphorus. Besides being good for your kidneys, it's also quite simple to prepare.

Ingredients:

- 1/2 chopped onion
- 1/2 chopped green bell pepper
- 1/4 cup sliced mushrooms
- 3 beaten eggs
- Olive oil/cooking spray
- Salt, and pepper to taste

Instructions:

Over medium heat, prepare the onions, bell peppers, mushrooms, salt, and black pepper in a large pan coated with oil or frying spray. Soften the veggies by cooking them for a while. Cook the eggs in a separate pan until they are set. Eat with a slice of low-phosphorus bread or whole-wheat toast.

A Berry Smoothy:

You should drink this smoothie every day because of its high vitamin and antioxidant content. A lack of potassium and phosphorus also characterizes it.

Ingredients:

- Almond milk or water
- 34 cup half a cup each of strawberries and blueberries
- 1/4 cup raspberries

Instructions:

Blenderize the whole lot until it's a uniform consistency. Quickly take pleasure in!

Low-Phosphorusola:

This granola will set you up for a successful day. It has a lot of protein and fiber but not a lot of phosphorus.

Ingredients:

Half a cup of rolled oats One-fourth cup of slivered almonds One-fourth cup of chopped walnuts One-eighth teaspoon of salt One-third cup of honey or agave nectar One-third cup of canola oil or olive oil

Instructions:

Set temperature to 325 degrees F (160 degrees C) and get ready to bake. Add the salt to the oats and mix in the nuts and almonds. Honey/agave nectar, oil, and vanilla extract should be combined in a separate basin. Put the liquids in a bowl and the dry ones in another. In a baking dish lined with parchment paper, spread the ingredients. Turn the pan over once halfway through the baking time. Upon completion of cooling, place the granola in an airtight container.

Some examples of breakfasts that are suitable for those on a renal diet are shown below. Creative cooking may still yield kidney-friendly dishes high in flavor and nutrients.

Chilli with Carne:

This chili has a healthy balance of protein, fiber, and carbs, and is light on sodium and potassium. Also, it's simple to whip up and keeps nicely in the freezer.

Ingredients:

- 1/2 chopped onion
- 1/4 cup chopped celery
- 1/4 cup chopped green bell pepper
- 1 28-ounce can diced tomatoes undrained
- 1 15-ounce can kidney beans
- 1 15-ounce can pinto beans
- 1 12-ounce can corn;

- 14 teaspoon each garlic powder and ground cumin; salt and pepper to taste

Instructions:

Add the onion, celery, bell pepper, tomatoes, kidney beans, pinto beans, corn, garlic powder, cumin, salt, and black pepper to a large saucepan or Dutch oven. Raise temperature to a boil over medium heat. Simmer at low heat for half an hour. Sour cream and shredded cheese are great additions (but not required). Enjoy!

Clearly, there are a wide variety of tasty dishes that are nonetheless kidney-friendly while adhering to a renal diet. Creative cooking may still yield kidney-friendly dishes high in flavor and nutrients.

In any case, there it is! Here are three breakfast options that adhere to the guidelines of the renal diet and will help you get off to a good start. In order to have enough energy to go through the day, it's crucial to start it off well with a healthy breakfast.

Enjoy your meal!

FRESH IDEAS FOR A RENAL DIET LUNCH

During the midday hours, sticking to a renal diet might be difficult. It's natural to want to know what tasty and nutritious options you have. Have a look at these delicious lunch ideas. This roasted red pepper soup dish is simple and delicious, making it a great choice for a quick lunch. The peppers' rich, complex taste is enhanced by roasting them before adding them to the soup's creamy base. Add some bread or crackers and you have a complete supper.

This lentil and vegetable stew dish is perfect for those cold winter nights. You can make a big batch on the weekend and have healthy, filling lunches for the whole week.

This salad, which has grilled chicken and avocado, is ideal if you're trying to cut back on your calorie intake. There's a lot of protein from the grilled chicken, and good fats from the avocado. Changing up the salad's components to suit personal preference is a breeze.

Whatever you decide, plan ahead and bring some snacks to keep you from going hungry in between meals. Delicious choices include trail mix, bananas, and yogurt. You won't have any problem sticking to your renal diet for lunch if you come prepared with one of these dishes.

How to Make Soup:

Including: Salad with Grilled Chicken and Avocado; Lentil and Vegetable Stew; and Roasted Red Pepper Soup

Tips:

Avoid becoming too hungry between meals by bringing some snacks with you, and try this savory and simple soup dish for lunch with roasted red peppers.

• This lentil and vegetable stew dish is perfect for those cold winter nights. You can make a big batch on the weekend and have healthy, filling lunches for the whole week.

• This salad, which has grilled chicken and avocado, is ideal if you're trying to cut back on your calorie intake. There's a lot of protein from the grilled chicken, and good fats from the avocado. Changing up the salad's components to suit personal preference is a breeze.

• Whatever you decide, plan ahead and bring some snacks to keep you from going hungry in between meals. Delicious choices include trail mix, bananas, and yogurt. You won't have any problem sticking to your renal diet for lunch if you come prepared with one of these dishes.

Recipe for Roasted Red Pepper Soup

The rich and smokey aromas of this Roasted Red Pepper Soup are a treat for the taste senses. Roasting the bright red bell peppers at the outset of this recipe gives the soup a delicious charred flavor. After being sautéed with onions and garlic, the peppers are then mixed with fragrant spices to create a rich and flavorful sauce foundation. Pureeing the ingredients and then boiling it with vegetable broth until it reaches a harmonic consistency creates a velvety texture. A little bit of cream is added to the soup to give it that extra special touch, making each mouthful rich and decadent. Lastly, a garnish of fresh herbs like parsley or basil adds a vivacious freshness that pairs wonderfully with the roasted pepper aromas. This recipe for Roasted Red Pepper Soup is likely to wow the taste buds of anybody who tries it, whether as a hearty first course or a filling main meal.

The ingredients are:

- 12 red bell peppers
- 1/4 cup olive oil

- Salt and pepper to taste
- 1/2 teaspoon sugar
- 1/8 teaspoon cayenne pepper (optional)
- 1/2 cup chopped onion
- 1/4 cup chopped celery
- 1/3 cup all-purpose flour
- 48 ounces chicken or vegetable broth

Method:

Set oven temperature to 375 degrees F. Peppers should be halved lengthwise, with the stems and seeds thrown away. Prepare a baking sheet by laying pepper halves skin-side up. Season with salt, pepper, sugar, and cayenne pepper (if using). Drizzle with olive oil. Leave in the oven for another 5 minutes if the skin is still wet. Take out of oven and cool for a while. Remove the stems and seeds from the peppers, then slice them into small pieces.

To soften the onions and celery, sauté them in the remaining oil in a large saucepan or Dutch oven over medium heat. After a minute or two, when the liquid is bubbling, stir in the flour and continue cooking. Peppers and broth should be added. Put on low heat and let simmer for 20 minutes. Using an immersion blender (or a conventional blender) and returning to the saucepan, puree the soup until smooth. If desired, season with more salt and pepper. Hot, with sour cream and croutons on the side, if you want.

The Best Lentil and Veggie Stew Ever!

This recipe for the Best Lentil and Veggie Stew Ever combines the healthy benefits of lentils with a colorful array of veggies to create a satisfying and delicious stew. Those looking for a healthy and filling supper will find this stew to be ideal. Vegetables contribute a wide variety of vitamins, minerals, and antioxidants, and lentils are a great source of plant-based protein and fiber. The long, slow simmering brings out all of the stew's savory aromas and mellow, satisfying tastes. The lentils and veggies are hearty, and the herbs and spices complement each other beautifully. This stew may be made with a wide variety of veggies and spices, making it not only tasty but also highly adaptable. The Best Lentil and Veggie Stew Ever is a crowd-pleaser that can be eaten as a hearty dinner or a filling lunch and will leave you feeling full and fed.

The ingredients are:

- 14 cup olive oil
- 12 cup chopped onion
- 12 cup chopped carrot
- 12 cup chopped celery
- Salt, and pepper to taste
- 13 cup all-purpose flour
- 64 ounces of chicken or vegetable broth
- 14 ounces of diced tomatoes
- 12 teaspoon dried thyme
- 12 teaspoon dried oregano
- 14 teaspoon cayenne pepper (optional), and 16 ounces of dry lentils, rinsed

Method:

Sauté chopped onions, carrots, and celery in olive oil in a large saucepan or Dutch oven over medium heat until tender.

Pepper and salt the food.

After a minute or two, when the liquid is bubbling, stir in the flour and continue cooking.

Mix in the tomato paste, broth, thyme, oregano, and cayenne pepper.

Put on low heat and let simmer for 20 minutes.

After adding the lentils, keep the pot on the stove for another 20-30 minutes.

If desired, season with more salt and pepper.

Sprinkle with cheese and/or sour cream and serve hot.

A Recipe for Chicken and Avocado Salad that Can Be Grilled

A grill or grill pan should be heated to medium-high temperatures before use. Season the chicken with the four spices: salt, pepper, chili powder, and cumin. Toss with olive oil and serve. To ensure even cooking, grill for a total of 12 minutes, turning once. Take off the grill, let it cool, and then cut it up into little pieces. In a large bowl, mix together the salad leaves, tomatoes, chicken, and avocado. To serve, drizzle with the dressing of your choice. Enjoy!

Ingredients:

- 12 ounces of chicken breasts, skin removed
- Salt and pepper to taste
- 1/2 teaspoon chili powder
- 1/4 teaspoon cumin; olive oil for grilling
- 12 cups of salad greens
- 1/2 cup diced tomatoes

Whatever you decide, plan ahead and bring some snacks to keep you from going hungry in between meals. Delicious choices include trail mix, bananas, and yogurt. Following your renal diet at lunch won't be a problem if you have these dishes on hand, and you can still enjoy your food without feeling deprived. Maintain your good health.

RECIPES FOR A RENAL DIET DINNER

Contrary to popular belief, a renal diet is not very restricted. Many mouthwatering dinners may be prepared using everyday items. Some of our favorites are listed here.

Broccoli with Chicken Alfredo:

This traditional meal is simple to prepare and works well with a kidney-friendly diet. After fully cooking the chicken breasts in olive oil, add the garlic and broccoli florets. Add some alfredo sauce from a jar and heat it up. You may choose to serve this dish over brown rice or whole wheat pasta.

Ingredients:

- Broccoli florets
- Chicken breasts
- Olive oil, garlic
- And alfredo sauce
- Pasta made with whole grains or brown rice (if desired)

Instructions:

Olive oil may be used to sauté chicken breasts until they are fully done. Put some broccoli florets and garlic in a pan and sauté them until they're soft. Heat up a jar of premade Alfredo sauce and pour it in. You may choose to serve this dish over brown rice or whole wheat pasta.

Salsa Verde Enchiladas with Carne:

There's a lot of protein and taste in these enchiladas. First, in a large pan, cook the ground beef over medium heat. Dice some onions and peppers and throw them in the pan to soften. Toss in an enchilada sauce jar and some chili powder. Wrap the meat filling in whole wheat tortillas and set them seam side down in a baking tray. Bake at 350 degrees until the cheese is melted and bubbling.

Ingredients:

- Lean chuck meat
- Onions Peppers
- Sauce for enchiladas
- Pepper powder
- Tostadas de trigo
- Crumbled cheese

Directions:

Brown the ground beef in a large pan over medium heat. To soften the onions and peppers, add them to the pan. Toss in an enchilada sauce jar and some chili powder. Roll up the whole wheat tortillas that you just filled with the beef mixture and set them seam side down in a baking tray. Bake at 350 degrees until the cheese is melted and bubbling. Enjoy!

Chicken Piccata:

This seafood recipe is so simple, it's ideal for a quick midweek dinner. Shrimp may be prepared quickly by sautéing them in olive oil and garlic, followed by adding white wine and a squeeze of lemon. Cook until shrimp are done, then stir in fresh parsley and serve over brown rice or whole-wheat pasta.

Ingredients:

- Shrimp
- Avocado oil
- Garlic
- Vin Gris
- Squeezed lemons
- Parsley
- Pasta made with whole wheat or brown rice

Directions:

Cook the shrimp in the olive oil and garlic over medium heat. Cook the white wine and lemon juice until the liquid is reduced by half in the pan. Add the chopped parsley and serve over brown rice or whole wheat pasta. Enjoy!

Bell Pepper Stuffing:

Stuffed bell peppers are a healthy and easy option for dinner throughout the week. Fill roasted bell peppers with ground turkey, diced tomatoes, black beans, corn, and salsa after tossing with olive oil and salt. Shredded cheese is added at the end and baked until it melts.

Ingredients:

- Chili peppers
- Avocado oil
- Salt
- Cured turkey meat
- Tomatoes, diced
- Beans, black
- Corn
- Salsa
- Crumbled cheese

Directions:

Put in a preheated 375 degree oven. Remove the stem and the seeds from the bell peppers. Roast for 25 minutes at 400 degrees, then season with olive oil and salt. Combine ground turkey with salsa, black beans, corn, chopped tomatoes, and sour cream. Sprinkle some shredded cheese on top before stuffing the mixture into the bell peppers. Continue baking for 15 minutes, or until melted.

Salad with kidney beans:

If you're hosting a summer BBQ or picnic, this kidney bean salad is a must-have. Kidney beans, tomatoes, cucumbers, green onions, and parsley are just some of the nutritious components that go into making this dish. Olive oil, white wine vinegar, and Dijon mustard form a tangy but mild vinaigrette dressing that is stirred with the salad.

Ingredients:

- Black-eyed peas
- Tomatoes
- Cucumbers
- Onions, green
- Parsley
- Avocado oil
- Vinegar from white wines
- Mustard with a Dijon twist

Directions:

In a large bowl, toss together the kidney beans, tomatoes, cucumbers, green onions, and parsley. In a little glass jar or dish, combine the olive oil, white wine vinegar, and Dijon mustard and whisk to combine. Toss the salad with the dressing and serve cold or at room temperature.

CHAPTER SEVEN

SNACK RECIPES FOR RENAL DIET

If you are following a renal diet, it is possible that you may need to restrict the quantities of certain foods and beverages that you consume. Foods that are rich in potassium, such as bananas, oranges, and tomatoes, are included in this category. It is possible that you may also need to reduce the amount of phosphorus-rich foods that you consume, such as dairy products, nuts, and seeds.

Consuming more snacks that are low in potassium and phosphorus may be an effective strategy for maintaining healthy levels of these minerals in the body. Try your hand at making any of these snack foods that are appropriate for a renal diet:

Edamame that's been roasted:

Edamame is a specific kind of green soybean that is often consumed in the form of a snack. Because it contains around 12 milligrams of potassium and 78 milligrams of phosphorus per cup, roasted edamame is an excellent choice for those who are following a renal diet.

Ingredients:

- Edamame Beans
- Olive oil
- Salt

Directions:

Prepare the oven to 375 degrees Fahrenheit by preheating it. Olive oil should be drizzled over the edamame pods that have been spread out on a baking pan. After sprinkling with salt, put the dish in the oven for 15 minutes, or until it has a golden brown color. Have some as a light snack!

Dip for Hummus:

Chickpeas, tahini, lemon juice, and garlic are the main ingredients in the Middle Eastern dip known as hummus. It is low in both potassium and phosphorus while having a high concentration of fiber and protein. Approximately 274 milligrams of potassium and 234 milligrams of phosphorus may be found in a single cup of hummus.

Ingredients:

One can of chickpeas, which is equivalent to 15 ounces.

A half cup's worth of tahini

One-quarter cup of lemon juice

Two individual garlic cloves

One and a half milligrams of ground cumin

To taste, salt and pepper is available.

Directions:

Put all of the ingredients in a food processor or a blender, and pulse them until they are completely smooth. If the hummus is too thick, add a little water at a time until it reaches the appropriate consistency. You may either keep it in the refrigerator for later use or serve it with crackers, pita bread, or veggies.

Chips made from vegetables:

The renal diet recommends vegetable chips as an alternative to potato chips because of the latter's higher potassium and phosphorus content. roughly 20 milligrams of potassium and roughly 80 milligrams of phosphorus may be found in an ounce serving of vegetable chips.

Ingredients:

- One pound of the veggies you like eating the most (for example, carrots, sweet potatoes, or zucchini).

- The olive oil
- To taste, salt and pepper is available.

Directions:

Prepare the oven to 375 degrees Fahrenheit by preheating it. After you have sliced the veggies as thinly as possible, sprinkle them with olive oil. After being seasoned with salt and pepper and placed in the oven, the food should be crisp after twenty minutes. Have some as a light snack!

Popcorn:

The amount of potassium and phosphorus that popcorn contains is rather modest. Approximately 55 milligrams of potassium and 100 milligrams of phosphorus may be found in one cup of popped corn.

Ingredients:

- A tablespoon's worth of kernels from popcorn
- One tablespoon of butter or olive oil is recommended, but not required.

Directions:

The popcorn kernels should be placed inside of a brown paper bag. After you have microwaved the bag for two to three minutes, or until the popcorn kernels have popped, fold the top of the bag over a few times to seal it. After removing it from the microwave, you may sprinkle it with butter or olive oil, if you so choose. Have some as a light snack!

Toasted Cucumber with Hummus:

This wholesome munch is a breeze to prepare and is loaded with all kinds of beneficial nutrients. Comparatively, the amount of potassium and phosphorus in one cup of cucumber is around 16 milligrams and 36 milligrams, respectively, whereas the amount of potassium and phosphorus in one quarter cup of hummus is approximately 26 milligrams and 72 milligrams, respectively.

Ingredients:

One cup of sliced cucumber, measured out.

A one-fourth cup serving of hummus

To taste, salt and pepper is available.

Directions:

Put the sliced cucumbers and hummus in a small bowl and mix them together. After you've seasoned it with salt and pepper, dig in!

Smoothie made with berries:

Make a berry smoothie if you want a delicious treat that is also low in phosphorus and potassium and is a good option for those seeking to lose weight. Just throw in your preferred fruit, some milk or yogurt, and ice, and mix until smooth. In comparison, one cup of blackberries has around 14 milligrams of potassium and 62 milligrams of phosphorus, whereas one cup of raspberries contains approximately 12 milligrams of potassium and 54 milligrams of phosphorus.

Ingredients:

One cup of either red or black raspberries or blackberries

One and a half cups of yogurt or milk.

Ice cubes may be added if desired.

Directions:

Enjoy the drink after pulverizing the ice, milk or yogurt, and raspberries to a smooth consistency.

CHAPTER EIGHT

RECIPES FOR DESSERT ON THE RENAL DIET

You may be surprised to learn that you don't have to give up your favorite desserts while on a renal diet. You may satisfy your sweet desire without jeopardizing your kidney health by making one of these delectable dessert recipes.

How to Make Chocolate Cake:

- 1/2 cup chocolate powder, unsweetened
- 14 cup of flour for all purposes
- baking soda, half a teaspoon
- a little salt
- 1/2 cup (or 1 stick) of room-temperature unsalted butter
- a quarter of a cup of sugar

- 1/4 cup of granulated light brown sugar 1 beaten egg
- 1/2 cup acidulated milk (such as buttermilk) 1 teaspoon vanilla essence

Method:

Turn oven temperature up to 350 degrees F. Coat an eight-inch cake pan with butter and flour. In a bowl, sift the dry ingredients (cocoa powder, flour, baking soda, and salt). In a separate dish, beat the sugar and butter until fluffy. Be sure to thoroughly mix the mixture after adding each egg. Add the dry ingredients to the creamed mixture first, followed by the wet components, and finishing with the dry ingredients. When the batter is smooth, add the buttermilk (or sour milk*) and the vanilla essence. Bake for 35 minutes, or until a toothpick inserted in the middle comes out clean, after pouring batter into the prepared pan. Allow cake to cool for 15 minutes in pan on wire rack before flipping onto serving platter. Top with whipped cream or your preferred dipping sauce.

Cherry Pie Recipe:

Ingredients:

- 2 ½ cups all-purpose flour
- 1 teaspoon salt
- 1 cup unsalted butter, cold and cut into small cubes
- ¼ to ½ cup ice water
- 4 cups fresh or frozen cherries, pitted
- 1 cup granulated sugar
- ¼ cup cornstarch
- 1 tablespoon lemon juice
- 1 teaspoon vanilla extract
- 1 tablespoon butter, for dotting
- 1 egg, beaten (for egg wash)
- 1 tablespoon granulated sugar (for sprinkling)

Instructions:

Preparing the Dough:

a. In a large bowl, combine the flour and salt. Add the cold butter cubes and use a pastry cutter or your hands to cut the butter into the flour until the mixture resembles coarse crumbs.

b. Gradually add the ice water, a few tablespoons at a time, while mixing the dough with a fork. Continue adding water and mixing until the dough comes together and forms a ball.

c. Divide the dough in half and shape each half into a disk. Wrap them in plastic wrap and refrigerate for at least 1 hour.

Preparing the Cherry Filling:

a. In a large bowl, combine the cherries, granulated sugar, cornstarch, lemon juice, and vanilla extract. Gently stir until the cherries are evenly coated. Let the mixture sit for about 15 minutes to allow the juices to release.

Preparing the Pie:

a. Preheat the oven to 425°F (220°C).

b. On a lightly floured surface, roll out one of the dough disks into a circle about 12 inches in diameter. Carefully transfer the rolled-out dough to a 9-inch pie dish and gently press it into the bottom and sides.

c. Pour the cherry filling into the pie crust, making sure it is evenly distributed.

d. Dot the top of the filling with small pieces of butter.

Assembling and Baking:

a. Roll out the second dough disk into a similar-sized circle. You can either place it on top of the filling as a full crust or cut it into strips to create a lattice pattern.

b. If using a full crust, make a few small slits on the top to allow steam to escape during baking. If creating a lattice pattern, arrange the strips in a crisscross pattern over the filling.

c. Brush the top crust (or lattice) with the beaten egg wash and sprinkle with granulated sugar.

d. Place the pie on a baking sheet to catch any drips and bake in the preheated oven for 15 minutes. Then, reduce the oven temperature to 375°F (190°C) and continue baking for an additional 40 to 45 minutes, or until the crust is golden brown and the filling is bubbling.

e. Once done, remove the pie from the oven and let it cool on a wire rack for at least 2 hours before serving.

Serving:

a. Slice the cherry pie into wedges and serve at room temperature or slightly warm.

b. Optional: Serve with a scoop of vanilla ice cream or a dollop of whipped cream for added indulgence. Enjoy your homemade cherry pie!

Banoffee Pie

Bananas, as you may know, are a good source of potassium. There is hardly any potassium in banana pudding (around 70 milligrams). However, if you make a gourmet banana pudding using real bananas, each dish might include an extra 100mg to 150mg of the drug.

Ingredients:

- 1/3 cup flour
- Half a cup of granulated sugar,
- A sprinkle of salt, eggs, milk that has been beaten, and an optional teaspoon of vanilla extract or banana extract
- slices of ripe banana (optional).

Method:

Put the cornstarch, sugar, and salt into a medium pot and stir to combine. Add the eggs and half of the milk, whisking constantly, until a smooth batter forms. Pour in the remaining milk and any extracts. Stir the mixture regularly while it cooks over medium heat until it reaches a boil. Take it off the fire and let it cool down a little. If used, line the bottom of a bowl with banana slices. Combine banana slices and pudding. Put it in the fridge for at least two hours before serving, covered.

Brownie-Making Instructions:

half a cup of melted unsalted butter (or one stick) 3/4 cup of white sugar 1/4 cup of packed light brown sugar eggs beaten to a foamy consistency

vanilla essence, half a teaspoon

1/4 cup self-rising flour

1/3 cup chocolate powder, unsweetened

Method:

Turn oven temperature up to 350 degrees F. Grease and flour a square baking dish, about eight inches in size.

In a large bowl, combine the sugar, butter, eggs, and vanilla extract and whisk until creamy.

Add the flour and cocoa powder through a sifter and stir until incorporated.

The cake is done when a toothpick inserted in the middle comes out clean, which usually takes approximately 25 minutes after pouring the mixture into the prepared pan.

Cut into squares while still warm, or let cool in the pan on a wire rack.

Nut-Based Sweets

Potassium is easily obtained through eating a piece of pie topped with cream or whipped cream. Pecan pie, a traditional American treat, is a good source of potassium. Pecans, like other nuts, have a lot of potassium. There are 162 milligrams of potassium in a serving of pecan pie (133 grams).

Ingredients:

- Pie crust (either handmade or store-bought) to make a two-crust pie.
- Granulated sugar, one cup
- All-purpose flour, seven table spoons
- Dollop of salt
- Two cups of corn syrup, light* three eggs, softly beaten
- Half a teaspoon of pure vanilla essence
- Two cups of chopped pecans; one pound of unsalted butter; use only when butter has cooled somewhat.

You may also use half-and-half, dark corn syrup, and chopped pecans. Preparation: set oven temperature to 375 degrees F (190 degrees C). Flour a work surface and roll out enough crust to line the bottom and up the sides of a nine-inch pie dish. Cut the pastry to fit into the container. For the topping, set aside 1/2 cup of the chopped pecans.

Combine the sugar, flour, and salt in a mixing bowl, then add the corn syrup, eggs, and vanilla. Blend the ingredients together after adding the butter. Fill a pie plate with crust and then pour in the filling. Place pecans you saved on top of the filling. In order to cover the pie, roll out the remaining dough. Wet the outside edge of the bottom crust and put it over the filling. Seal with artistic crimping and steam vents cut into top crust. Bake for 50 minutes at 375 degrees Fahrenheit (190 degrees Celsius).

CHAPTER NINE

MEAL PLANNING AND GROCERY SHOPPING TIPS FOR THE RENAL DIET.

Meal planning and grocery shopping may be tough regardless of whether you have just been diagnosed with renal disease or have been managing it for some time. But there are several things you can do to make the process simpler and less intimidating, and you can do all of this while still maintaining a renal diet that is not only healthy but also tasty.

Preparing as many of your meals as advance as you can is another essential piece of advice. If you plan ahead and make some of your meals in advance, you will be able to guarantee that you have some nutritious alternatives accessible even when you are pressed for time or just don't feel like cooking. Dishes that are simple to prepare and suitable for a renal diet include lentil soup, grilled salmon, roasted veggies, and quinoa bowls.

When going grocery shopping when following a renal diet, it is vital to choose foods that are low in phosphorus, potassium, and salt. The best food options are fresh fruits and vegetables, lean protein sources like chicken and fish, and cereals in their entire form. Make it a habit to examine the nutrition facts shown on food labels, and cut down on your consumption of processed foods that are high in salt and include other harmful substances.

Another essential piece of advice is to center your diet as much as possible on fresh foods. The renal diet benefits greatly from the inclusion of fresh fruits and vegetables, lean protein sources such as chicken or fish, and complete grains. When you go to the grocery store, make an effort to buy less processed food that is high in salt and contains other components that are bad. If you keep these guidelines in mind, you will be well on your way to consuming a renal diet that is not only tasty but also full of essential nutrients. Experiment with a variety of recipes and concepts for meals until you discover those that are suitable for you and the way you live your life. Also, keep in mind that dealing with kidney illness is a journey; thus, you should do things one step at a time.

On a renal diet, here are some things to keep in mind while planning meals and going grocery shopping:

Prepare yourself. You may save time and money by planning your meals for the week, and it will also be simpler for you to keep to your renal diet if you do this. First, write down all of the recipes you want to use for the next week's worth of meals, and then develop a shopping list based on those meal plans. Planning ahead can also help you avoid making hurried excursions to the grocery store or dining out, both of which often result in less healthful food selections.

Keep to the fundamental building blocks. If at all feasible, you should try to limit your diet to fundamental foods such as rice, beans, poultry, fish, and vegetables. These meals are simple to prepare in the kitchen and are straightforward to modify so that they conform to a renal diet.

Avoid foods that have been processed. It might be difficult for someone following a renal diet to steer clear of processed meals since they often include high levels of salt and other unhealthful substances. You should make an effort to cut down as much as you can on the amount of processed foods you eat. Carefully read all of the labels. When you go grocery shopping, you should always be sure to read the labels very carefully to verify that the food you buy is appropriate for a renal diet. Take note of the amounts of sodium, potassium, and phosphorus that are included in each food item.

Be sure to include some food. When following a renal diet, it is crucial to have nutritious snacks accessible, and this is particularly true if you have a tendency to grow hungry in between meals. Pick healthy snacks like fruits and vegetables, yogurt with less fat, or crackers made with whole grains.

Visit a dietician. If you are having difficulty sticking to a renal diet on your own, it may be beneficial to speak with a dietitian about your options. A dietician can assist you in developing a meal plan that caters to your individual requirements and interests, as well as provide advice on how you may adhere to your renal diet while still taking pleasure in the foods you consume.

It is not necessary for adhering to a renal diet for it to be difficult or laborious. You can prepare meals that are both good for you and tasty if you just put in a little bit of extra work and forethought. In addition, with the assistance of a dietician, you will be able to ensure that your renal diet is carefully designed to meet your needs. Therefore, if you feel that you are in need of assistance, do not be afraid to ask for it; there are a lot of tools available that may make adhering to a renal diet simple and fun.

If preparing meals from scratch is intimidating or takes a lot of time for you, seek for recipes that are fast and simple to make and involve a small number of ingredients and procedures.

Cooking bigger meals, then dividing them up into smaller portions and storing them in the freezer might be another way to save time. This way, you won't ever be caught without a nutritious dinner, and the preparation time will be kept to a minimum.

When going out to dine, you should always inquire about the components used in each dish, as well as whether or not the meal may be altered to accommodate a renal diet. Don't be hesitant to inquire about the restaurants' ability to accommodate particular dietary requirements; in fact, the majority of restaurants are more than pleased to do so, and many of them now feature selections that are safe for kidney patients on their menus.

Maintain proper control of your blood sugar

People who have diabetes or another disorder that generates substantial blood sugar levels are more likely to have damage to their kidneys. When your cells are unable to make use of the glucose (sugar) that is present in your blood, your kidneys are forced to exert more effort to filter it out. This may result in serious kidney damage over time owing to the pressure of day-to-day activities like eating and drinking, which can accelerate the process.

If you want to maintain your kidneys healthy, it is very necessary to keep a careful eye on your blood sugar levels and to take measures to keep them within a normal range. The renal diet, also known as a kidney diet, is one that may assist you in accomplishing this goal by offering meals that are lower in sugar and easier for your kidneys to digest.

There are additional things you may do to assist keep your blood sugar under control, in addition to following a renal diet, which is one of them:

• Using a glucose meter to keep a close eye on your blood sugar levels at regular intervals

• Taking blood sugar-regulating medicine as suggested by your physician

• consuming well-balanced meals at regular intervals and on a daily basis; engaging in regular physical activity; avoiding sugary foods and beverages.

It is imperative that you discuss a renal diet with your physician if you have diabetes or any illness that increases the likelihood of kidney damage occurring in your body. They will be able to give you precise recommendations on what foods to consume and how much of them, as well as propose drugs for you if they feel it is necessary. You can keep your blood sugar under control and prevent your kidneys from additional damage if you manage your condition carefully. This will enable you to enjoy a life that is both healthy and active.

CONCLUSION

The renal diet may be complicated, particularly when one first begins following it. To make the procedure less difficult for you, we have included a few recipes and helpful hints that you may use. Do not be hesitant to get in touch with one of our professionals if you have any queries or if you want more guidance. Today we will go over some of the fundamentals of the renal diet, including the items that should be consumed and those that should be avoided. In addition to that, we will provide you the recipe for a handmade kidney-friendly soup. People who suffer from chronic kidney disease (CKD) may benefit from following a renal diet, which is intended to help them maintain their health and avoid additional damage to their kidneys. In the absence of treatment, chronic kidney disease (CKD) is a degenerative condition that raises the risk of developing heart failure, stroke, and even death. If you have been told that you have CKD, beginning a renal diet as soon as you can after receiving this diagnosis is very vital.

There are certain fundamental recommendations that everyone need to follow, even if the particulars of the diet will change based on the circumstances of each individual.

Avoiding meals that are heavy in salt and phosphorus should be your first and primary priority. These minerals, when consumed over a period of time, might cause harm to the kidneys and raise the chance of developing difficulties. Foods that have been processed, foods stored in cans, and meals served in restaurants are all common sources of salt. Phosphorus may be present in a variety of foods, including dairy products, meat, nuts, and legumes. You not only need to stay away from foods that are rich in salt and phosphorus, but you also need to make sure that you are receiving enough protein and calcium in your diet. Calcium is important for bone health, while protein is necessary for the maintenance of both muscle mass and strength. Fish, poultry, lean meat, and eggs are all excellent choices for protein sources. Along with other calcium-rich meals like cereal and orange juice, dairy products are an excellent supply of this mineral. Finding dishes that are both nutritious and appetizing might be one of the most difficult aspects of adhering to a renal diet. For this reason, we have compiled this renal diet cookbook for those just starting out. All of the recipes included in this book are simple to put together and are kidney-friendly. We have high hopes that you will find these recipes to be useful and that they will make it a little bit simpler for you to adhere to your renal diet. Do not be hesitant to get in touch with one of our professionals if you have any queries or if you want more guidance.

Made in the USA
Las Vegas, NV
13 January 2024

84312780R00052